You'll have loads of fun making this delicious house from graham crackers, icing and candies. It will be a big hit!

1. Use melted chocolate to join graham cracker rectangles together.

2. Center horizontal cracker above others. Make two.

3. Using pattern, cut eaves. Be careful not to break graham crackers.

4. Use icing to attach M&Ms to roof.

5. Use icing to create vines, door frame and wreath.

Gram's House sooo yummy!

GRAM'S HOUSE INGREDIENTS:

2 boxes Graham crackers (20 whole, 2 halves)
20 honey Grahams Sticks
Two 15 ounce package M&Ms (Yellow, Red and Orange)
¼ cup White chocolate
½ cup light or dark chocolate
½ package Yellow chocolate
1 can Yellow icing
1 can Red icing

1 can Orange icing
1 can Green icing
4 peppermint sticks
4 peppermint drops
9 Red Twizzler Sticks

TIP: Use warm chocolate to glue pieces together throughout. Work on waxed paper.

6. Ice window panes, frame with colored icing.

7. Vary your windows for added interest.

HOUSE PATTERN

PREPARATION:
Floor: Join 3 whole crackers, long sides touching. Let chocolate cool until very firm. Turn over, lay a row of Graham sticks flat, end to end, on 1st 3, touching all 4 edges. Attach to strengthen base of house.
Front & Back Walls: Join 3 whole crackers together, long sides touching. Center 4th cracker sideways along top edge of walls, join. Using pattern, cut peak and wall shapes. Make 2.
Side Walls: Join 2 whole crackers together with the long sides touching.
Roof: Join 3 whole crackers together, long sides touching. Make 2.
Door: One cracker to be added at assembly.
Windows: One half cracker each for 3 windows, half 1 Graham stick lengthwise to fashion shutters, add at assembly.

ASSEMBLY:
Attach side walls horizontally. Apply chocolate to edge of 1 side wall, attach to edge of front wall. Attach 2nd side wall to front, side walls to back wall. Stand joined walls on waxed paper, squaring all corners. Let dry thoroughly. A box is helpful to keep walls upright until dry. Spread chocolate on top edge of all walls, attach roof panels. Spread Yellow chocolate on roof and door cracker. Attach M&Ms to roof icing while still soft. If icing hardens too quickly, dip M&Ms in warm chocolate, then apply. Spread White chocolate on window crackers, add sprinkles. Draw panes on windows with Yellow icing. Let dry. Spread chocolate on back of window and door crackers. Attach windows to side and back walls, centering. Center door on front wall, attach. Let dry. Use decorator tips and icing to draw details on house, see pictures. Apply Twizzler sticks, peppermint sticks and drops as desired.

Fold

Combine basic craft supplies, candy and creativity to make great treats for every occasion. Just follow our never-fail instructions for terrific results every time.

Happy Easter

Chocolate Filled Egg: Gently crack the top of an egg, empty and wash thoroughly. Rub your finger along inside to gently peel away skin lining the eggshell. Dry thoroughly. Fill with chocolate.

Alternately, butter inside of cleaned eggshell half and sit upright in an egg carton. Following directions for painting with chocolate, paint inside of shell with White chocolate, paint several layers to mimic egg white. Fill center with yellow chocolate or yellow crème filling.

Just for Dad - For Father's Day or the big game, serve Dad dipped pretzels in a bag or give him Moose Munch in a tub. To make Moose Munch, follow directions for clustered nuts, substituting toffee popcorn or Cracker Jacks for nuts, coat with chocolate.

Christmas - Chocolate molded into wreaths, bells and stars will liven up your holiday buffet table. Add some candy cane reindeer and you're all set.

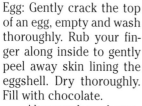

Halloween Ghost Pops - A new spin on an old treat. Wrap a lollipop with tissue, cover with organza fabric. Tie with satin ribbon. Hole punch black cardstock for eyes and glue onto fabric.

Winter Treats in a Bag - Simpler than a canning jar, cut your cocoa or cookie in a jar recipe by one third and layer in a clear cone shaped icing bag. Add cute ribbons, miniatures and even rub-ons to embellish.

Valentine's Day - Simple ready-made candies can be used in creative ways to make special cards and decorations.

Wedding and Shower Favors - Jordan almonds, available in craft and party stores, are a traditional wedding favor candy. Simply place candy coated almond in an organza bag and add a millinery flower.

Melting Chocolate

With double boiler pans over a hot stove, melting chocolate was once a tricky endeavor. Now, all you need is a microwave oven for fast and easy melting.

TIPS: Never let melted chocolate contact water. It will cause the chocolate to immediately harden or become thick. You cannot remelt and use chocolate that has been in contact with water. • Do not overheat chocolate. It will become thick and unworkable.

BASIC MELTING INSTRUCTIONS:

Modern Method - Pour about 6 ounces of Guittard melting chocolate wafers in a microwave-safe bowl. Melt at 50% power or defrost for 1 minute at a time, stirring in between. Continue until melted and smooth, with no trace of wafer chunks.

1. Pour 6 ounces of chocolate wafers into a microwave-safe bowl.

2. Heat at 50% power for 1 minute, stir. Wafers will begin to melt.

3. Heat at 1 minute intervals, stirring until wafers are completely melted.

Creative Techniques

Painting

1. Melt chocolate colors separately. Use 1 candy paintbrush per color. Allow to dry before adding next color.

2. After painting, fill mold with your base, usually milk or White chocolate.

Layering

1. Put first layer into mold, chill or allow to dry.

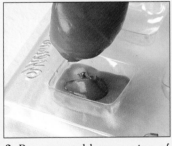

2. Pour second layer on top of first. A different color, flavor or texture will add interest to your candy.

Marbleizing

1. Melt 2 or more colors of wafers separately. Pour into your mold.

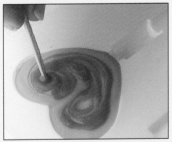

2. Gently swirl colors together in mold using a skewer or lollipop stick.

Drizzling

1. Use a teaspoon or cone bag to drizzle another color of chocolate on your creations.

2. For a different effect, drizzle in a second direction.

3. Drizzle additional colors for added interest.

PAINTING: You can add flair and dimension to your chocolates by using several colors. Melt different colors of chocolates separately. With a candy paintbrush, paint your mold. Do not use water to rinse, have several brushes handy. Each color should dry before the next is added to prevent running. You can then fill the mold with your base, usually milk or white chocolate.

LAYERING: You can pour different colors of chocolate in your mold to make a layered effect. Allow each layer to dry or chill before adding the next.

MARBLEIZING: Melt two or more colors of wafers separately, then combine in your mold. Gently swirl together using a skewer or lollipop stick. Don't swirl too much or colors will blend entirely, producing a whole new color.

DRIZZLING: You can use a teaspoon, cone bag or bottle to drizzle another color of chocolate onto your creations. Use swift back and forth hand motions to avoid glopping on the chocolate. Create the effect of thin scribbled lines.

Dipped Chocolate

Nothing says "I love you" like a gift of chocolate. The ideas on these pages will help you create prized confections for special occasions and the special people in your life. But never forget that you, the creator, are the most special of all!

1. Wash and dry fruit thoroughly before dipping.

2. Hold leaf end of strawberry and dip.

3. After dipping, place strawberries on baking sheet lined with parchment or waxed paper. Refrigerate until firm.

4. For added flair, drizzle with another color chocolate or paint on a cute tuxedo bow.

Spring and early summer, bring on the fresh berries. Dipped strawberries make a great dessert, hostess gift, or a simple addition to a summer potluck. Keep stems and leaves on for a fancier appearance. Make sure berries are plump and juicy.

Dipped Strawberries - Wash fruit, dry thoroughly. Hold firmly, dip in melted chocolate. If chocolate layer in bowl is shallow, use a spoon to help coat berries. Place on baking sheet lined with parchment or wax paper. Refrigerate until firm. For added flair, drizzle with a different color of chocolate or paint a cute tuxedo bow onto dipped fruit.

Use jumbo pretzel sticks in pretzel molds or looped pretzels dipped and drizzled. Make batches in different colors for special occasion treats, Red & Green for Christmas, Pink, Blue & White for a baby shower. Or, choose your favorite team colors!

Dipped Pretzels - Dip pretzel into the melted chocolate. If necessary, use a spoon to help cover. Add sprinkles if desired. Place on baking sheet lined with parchment or wax paper. Refrigerate until firm. For added flair, drizzle with additional colors of chocolate.

1. Jumbo pretzel sticks are the best choice for dimensional molds, or just dip and drizzle. Hold and dip pretzel in melted chocolate.

2. Make batches different colors for special occasions - Red & Green for Christmas, pastels for Easter or a baby shower.

1. Fill cookie cutters halfway with melted chocolate.

2. Add embellishments like nuts and sprinkles.

Cookie Cutter Pop-Outs

Cookie-cutters as molds are fun to use. Leave your candy in or pop it out!

Place clean dry cookie cutters on a wax paper lined cookie sheet. Fill with melted chocolate halfway. You can add embellishments like nuts or sprinkles while chocolate is still warm. Carefully place in refrigerator for an hour. Do not jiggle the candies, moving cookie cutters too soon may cause chocolate to ooze out of shape. Wrap in cello bag with cookie cutter still attached or pop out of cookie cutter and wrap.

Cow Pies - Nothing says "home on the range" quite like a cow pie! Make a chocolate cow pie using a round cookie cutter and melted chocolate loaded with nuts.

Dipped Candy Sticks - Hard candy sticks or canes are great for dipping. You can layer to create greater thicknesses of chocolate or different layers of color.

Fill chocolate molds for an added surprise or use a candy dipping tool to simply dip the filling in chocolate for a free-form shape.

Using Molds

1. Melt chocolate in microwave using a special melting bottle from your craft store.

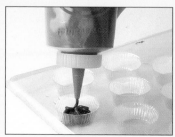

2. Fill mold directly from melting bottle.

3. Tap gently to remove air bubbles and chill.

Lusciously Delicious Dimensional Chocolates

Crème Centers

1. Fill your mold a little less than half full with chocolate.

2. Use a candy brush to generously paint the sides of the mold to the top with chocolate.

3. Fill with candy crème center. This can be bought in tubes at your craft store.

4. Fill remainder of mold with chocolate to seal in filling.

5. Tap gently to remove air bubbles and chill.

Many people who feel comfortable making fudge or dropped candy hesitate at the idea of using molds, adding crème centers or painting with chocolate. Follow our simple instructions and the mystery will disappear. Release your creativity and enjoy.

Nut Centers - Fill mold halfway with chocolate. Add nut to the center of the cavity. Almonds, walnuts, peanuts, macadamia nuts, etc. may be used. Chill to set. Fill the rest of the mold with chocolate. Gently tap mold to remove air bubbles and chill.

TIP: When hiding nuts in chocolate, tell guests or gift recipients. Many people are allergic to nuts.

Nut Centers

1. Half fill mold with chocolate. Add nut center to cavity.

2. Fill to top with chocolate. Tap to remove air bubbles.

Clustered Nuts - Drop unsalted nuts into melted chocolate. Your ratio should be even or more chocolate than nuts. Stir to completely coat nuts with chocolate. Remove 1 teaspoon of cluster at a time, drop in clumps on a wax paper covered baking sheet. Chill.

Old Fashioned Peanut Butter Cups - Buy peanut butter cup molds at your local craft store or roll filling into a ball. Use a candy dipping tool to dip into chocolate. For filling, mix 1 cup butter or margarine, 2 cups White sugar, and 7 ounces smooth peanut butter. Yields 20-30 small peanut butter cups.

Dressing up Baked Goods - You can dip cookies, rice krispie treats and dessert bars in chocolate. Don't forget to drizzle, add sprinkles or nuts on top for extra fun!

Molded Lollipops & More!

For special party favors, put the top of a plastic toy ring into each mold before the hard candy sets. Kids will love wearing edible jewelry.

1. Combine sugar, syrup and water in saucepan.

2. Stir until sugar is no longer gritty and mixture is smooth.

3. Place candy thermometer in saucepan and boil on medium heat until mixture reaches 300°.

4. Butter the molds.

5. Pour candy mixture into several containers for coloring.

6. Add colors and flavoring to the bowls. Mix well.

7. With a spoon, carefully pour hot mixture into molds.

8. Add sticks and rings to make candy novelties.

Yummy Lollipops on Parade

TIPS: Most of these candies are made with sugar syrups and require the use of a candy thermometer. Always check your thermometer before using it by placing it in a pot of boiling water. It should read 212°F. If it does not, take this difference into account when testing your syrups. • Work fast as candy mixtures set quickly. • If wrapping your finished product, use special bags that will not stick to your candy. Candy making suppliers should carry these.

Molded lollipops are so easy to create! Make the recipe, ready the mold, mix colors and pour. Add the stick handles and you have yourself a lollipop!

This is a great project to get your whole family involved in. Or, teach your girl scouts and boy scouts to make candy. Believe me, they will be interested!

HARD CANDY RECIPE

INGREDIENTS:
2 cups sugar
1 cup water
⅔ cup light corn syrup
1 teaspoon oil flavoring
   available at drugstores and
   baking supply shops
Food coloring as desired

SUPPLIES:
Candy molds
Lollipop sticks
Candy bags
Small heat safe bowls
   (Corning Ware or Pyrex)
Spoons
Saucepan with lid
Candy thermometer

PREPARATION:
In a heavy saucepan, mix sugar, water and syrup until sugar is dissolved. Boil over medium heat to 300°F or hard ball stage. Remove from heat.
Add flavoring and food coloring, mix well. Carefully but working quickly, pour hot mixture into buttered molds. A spoon works well for this step. Unmold when completely cool. Decorate if desired. Yields 1 pound.

BAKED APPLES

INGREDIENTS FOR BAGS:
Bag 1 contains spice mix:
½ cup commercial spice cake mix from a box
Bag 2 contains topping:
⅓ cup powdered sugar
2 tablespoons chopped walnuts

INSTRUCTIONS FOR TAG:
In a small bowl, combine spice mix, 1 egg yolk, 1 tablespoon vegetable oil and 1½ tablespoons water. Mix thoroughly.

Slice top off apple, core. Pour cake mixture into apple. Lightly spray plate with cooking spray, place apple on plate. Microwave on high for 2 minutes or until apple is cooked through. Let stand for 2 minutes.

In a small bowl, stir topping mix with 1 to 2 teaspoons water. With a fork poke several holes in top of cake, drizzle topping on cake. Enjoy!

For a gift, wrap one large apple, a bag of spice mix and a bag of glaze topping mix in a gift container. Your tag will tell the recipient how to make an easy apple muffin treat!

1. Core apple.

Apple Goodies

CARAMEL APPLES

TIP: Bring apples to room temperature so they do not perspire, allowing caramel to adhere properly.

INGREDIENTS:
Red or green apples
Caramel squares
Chopped peanuts, mini chocolate chips, or other topping

SUPPLIES:
Popsicle or cookie sticks
Wax paper
Microwave safe bowl
Spoon

PREPARATION:
Wash and dry apples thoroughly. Insert stick in bottom and set aside.
In microwave safe dish, melt caramel squares as you would chocolate wafers for 1 minute at a time on 50% power, stirring in between or according to the directions on the package.
Stir frequently, add more caramels as existing ones melt.
Spread wax paper on cookie sheet to protect countertop from heat.
Dip apple, stick side up in bowl of caramel. Use a spoon to cover top areas.
On separate sheet of wax paper, sprinkle toppings. Roll apple in topping while caramel is still warm.
Refrigerate on a wax paper lined cookie sheet. When cool, wrap in a cello bag.

2. Put filling into apple.

3. Add topping to cooked apple.

1. Dip apple, stick side up, in a bowl of warm melted caramel.

What could be better than yummy sweets that are good for you. Make up a batch and surprise the family. Or, better yet, let them help out!

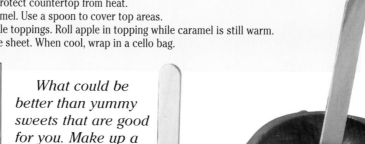

2. Roll apple in nuts or candies while caramel is still warm.

Mouth-Watering Cookie Pops

Most any cookie recipe or even Rice Krispie treats can be used to make cookie pops. All you need is a Wilton cookie pop mold and some long lollipop sticks. A little icing lets you get creative.

COOKIE POPS

INSTRUCTIONS:

Grease the inside of mold with butter or oil. Press cookie dough into mold to half full. Add the lollipop stick and almost fill with dough.

Bake at 350° for about 10 minutes, oven temperatures may vary.

Let cool before popping out of mold. Ice and embellish.

Carefully wrap cookie in a cello bag, tie with ribbon.

ICING:

Tubes of gel and cream icing are available in most craft and grocery stores. Wilton has introduced spray can icing with 4 different decorator tips. Use these decorating aids to add personal touches to your cookie pops.

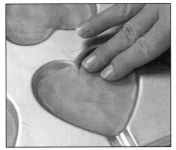

1. Press half of cookie dough into mold.

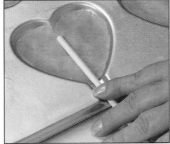

2. Place pop stick on dough.

3. Cover stick with second half of cookie dough.

4. Bake, cool and decorate finished cookie pop for a special occasion treat.

Kool-Aid Concoction

1. Layer sugars and Kool-Aid drink mix in jar. All layers should show on sides.

2. Top off with firmly packed lemon drops or delicious sugared orange slices.

3. Embellish the jar with paper umbrella and gift tag.

☉ther Unique Treats

KOOL-AID CONCOCTION

INGREDIENTS:
2½ cup White sugar
3 small packets unsweetened Kool-Aid drink mix
½ cup baker's sugar, Light Brown color
1 cup+ lemon drops or
1 cup+ candy Orange slices

SUPPLIES:
1 canning jar with lid
5" to 6" fabric square
Festive drink umbrella or candy necklace
Gift tag
Ribbon or yarn tie

INSTRUCTIONS: In jar, layer 1 cup White sugar then all the Kool-Aid. Use finger to push mix to sides of jar. All layers should show on outside. Add ½ cup White sugar, ½ cup baker's sugar and 1 cup White sugar. Fill remainder of jar with packed lemon drops or Orange slices. Screw on lid.
PREPARATION: Add cool water and ice to make 6 quarts. Will serve about 24.
FINISHING TOUCH: Write preparation instructions on tag. Cover lid with fabric square, secure with tie. Attach umbrella or candy necklace and tag.

Take some glassware and a little bit of creativity, and you can make fun treats out of almost any food or drink. Make it cute, make it festive and give instructions for completing the project.

Cinnamon Hot Cocoa Treat
In a small jar, layer 1 single serving packet of instant hot cocoa mix, chocolate chips and cinnamon chips (in baking section of grocery store). Gift tag will instruct to combine this mixture with hot milk or water in jumbo sized mug for a warming drink.

COLORED POPCORN

INGREDIENTS:
Unpopped popcorn
Wilton icing tint

SUPPLIES:
Zip lock baggie
Wax paper
Spatula
Butter knife
Brown paper lunch sack
Yarn or ribbon and tag

INSTRUCTIONS: Pour kernels into zip lock bag. Dip tip of a knife into tint, smear small amount of color on inside of bag. Too much color will make kernels wet and they will stick to inside of bag. Experiment with ratios to find color intensity you like. Seal bag, shake, rubbing bag between palms to evenly distribute color. Make several color batches. Shake onto wax paper, spread out with spatula. Let dry for several hours. Color may be somewhat tacky, try not to handle kernels. Use a funnel to layer into glass bottles.
TO POP: Place ¼ cup kernels in paper sack. Fold down top 3 times to secure. Place in microwave, pop on high for about 2 minutes, until frequency between pops is no longer than 2 seconds. Corn will be white with specks of subtle color. Yields about 5 cups popped.
FINISHING TOUCH: Attach tie, ornament and gift tag with popping instructions.

☉ookies in a ᒍar

CHOCOLATE CHIP COOKIE MIX

INGREDIENTS FOR JAR:
½ cup White sugar
½ cup chopped walnuts
1 cup chocolate chips
1 cup Brown sugar

2¼ cups flour mixture below:
2 cups White flour
1 teaspoon baking soda
Pinch of salt

SUPPLIES:
1 quart jar with lid
5" to 6" fabric square
Yarn or ribbon tie
Gift tag

INSTRUCTIONS: Layer ingredients in jar. Screw on lid.
FINISHING TOUCH: Gift tag will read as follows: Preheat oven to 350°. Mix dry ingredients in large bowl. Add 1 cup butter, 2 eggs and 1 teaspoon vanilla. Mix thoroughly. Drop heaping tablespoons, 1" between them, onto lightly greased cookie sheet. Bake for 10-15 minutes or until edges are browned. Yields 3 to 4 dozen. Cover lid with fabric square, secure with tie and attach tag.

M&M COOKIE MIX

INGREDIENTS FOR JAR:
1¼ cup White sugar
1 cup M&Ms candies
2 cups flour mixture:
2 cups White flour
½ teaspoon baking soda
½ teaspoon baking powder

SUPPLIES:
1 quart jar with lid
5" to 6" fabric square
Yarn or ribbon tie
Gift tag

INSTRUCTIONS: Layer ingredients in jar. Screw on lid.
FINISHING TOUCH: Gift tag will read as follows: Preheat oven to 375°. Mix dry ingredients in large bowl. Add ¾ cup butter, 2 eggs, 1 teaspoon vanilla. Mix. Drop heaping tablespoons onto lightly greased cookie sheet. Bake 10-15 minutes, until edges are browned. Yields 3 dozen. Cover lid with fabric, secure with tie and attach tag.

Christmas Corn
Place ¼ cup of kernels in a brown paper sack. fold over to seal. Pop in the microwave for about 1½ minutes. Enjoy!

SPOOKY POPCORN
¼ cup of kernels in a brown sack. fold to seal. Cook in microwave about 1½ minutes.

Kool-Aid Concoction

Cookie mix in a jar makes a gift that pleases twice, when received and when baked. A quart wide-mouth jar is a good choice for these recipes. Use a canning funnel to fill jars and a tart tamper or spoon to pack down mix as you add each layer. Packing down is an important step. Fill in order listed. Add raisins here, subtract nuts. Using these recipes as a guide, release your creativity and head for the kitchen!

SPICED OATMEAL RAISIN COOKIE MIX

INGREDIENTS FOR JAR:
¾ cup Brown sugar
½ cup White sugar
½ cup raisins
1¾ cups oats

1 cup+ flour mixture:
1 cup White flour
1 teaspoon cinnamon
½ teaspoon nutmeg
1 teaspoon baking soda

SUPPLIES:
1 quart canning jar with lid
5" to 6" fabric square
Yarn or ribbon tie
Gift tag

INSTRUCTIONS: Layer ingredients in jar. Screw on lid.
FINISHING TOUCH: Gift tag will read as follows: Preheat oven to 350°. Mix dry ingredients in large bowl. Add ¾ cup butter, 2 eggs, 1 teaspoon vanilla. Mix. Drop heaping tablespoons onto lightly greased cookie sheet. Bake 10-15 minutes, until edges are browned. Yields 3 dozen. Cover lid with fabric, secure with tie and attach tag.

PEANUT BUTTER COOKIE MIX

INGREDIENTS FOR JAR:
¾ cup chopped peanuts
¾ cup brown sugar
¾ cup white sugar
¾ cup peanut butter chips

1½ cups flour mixture below:
1½ cups White flour
1 teaspoon baking soda
Pinch of salt

SUPPLIES:
1 quart jar with lid
5" to 6" fabric square
Yarn or ribbon tie
Gift tag

INSTRUCTIONS: Layer ingredients in jar. Screw on lid.
FINISHING TOUCH: Gift tag will read as follows: Preheat oven to 350°. Mix dry ingredients in large bowl. Add ½ cup butter, ½ cup creamy peanut butter, 2 eggs and 1 teaspoon vanilla. Mix thoroughly. Drop heaping tablespoons, 1" between them, onto lightly greased cookie sheet. Bake for 10-15 minutes or until edges are browned. Yields 3 dozen. Cover lid with fabric square, tie and attach tag.

Simply S'Mores!

Camping trips with the family, scout outings and bar-beques in the back yard. Making S'Mores will bring back memories of fun times and days gone by. Whip up a batch of nostalgia with these clever ideas. Add a pinch of your own creativity, sit back and enjoy!

S'Mores in a Jar - Unassembled S'Mores in a cute jar? Make this clever idea your own. Layer broken chocolate bar, marshmallows and broken graham crackers. Use as a decoration or spray a pan with Pam, add contents and toast until slightly melted. Makes a sticky, gooey, yummy treat!

S'Mores in a Sack - Give S'Mores to go with this cute kit idea. In a brown handled kraft bag, place individual zip lock bags of jumbo marshmallows, chocolate bar chunks and graham crackers. Make a tiny clothes hanger from floral wire for toasting marshmallows. On the tag, instruct recipient to find the nearest campfire or microwave on a plate for 10 seconds for an instant treat.

Dipped Spoons - Chocolate dipped spoons are great for stirring coffee and cocoa. Dip a spoon in melted chocolate, try different flavors. Dip several times to build up thickness of chocolate, hold for 1 minute. Use colorful plastic spoons and package in small bags. Candy grade bags won't stick to chocolate. To use them as party favors, add a bow or cover bag with tulle.

1. Dip the spoon into the melted chocolate.

2. Add the miniature marshmallows while the chocolate is still warm.

S'Mores Spoons - Dip plastic spoon in melted chocolate. Decorate with mini marshmallows. Place in cellophane bag with a graham cracker. Attach single serving packet of hot cocoa mix. The recipient can make a cup of cocoa and stir it with the S'More spoon. The chocolate will melt and the marshmallows will liven up the cup. Make several, place in a mug for a charming gift.

Edible S'Mores Ornaments

1. Use melted chocolate dabs for eyes and nose to create a simple face.

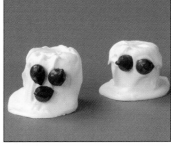

2. Slightly melt the marshmallows and you have cute ghost s'mores.

3. Add a hat and candy cane for a Santa s'more.

There are hundreds of ideas for making personalized and edible S'Mores ornaments. Make traditional holiday critters like snowmen, reindeer and sleigh riders. Candy buttons dipped in chocolate make great noses, dipped pieces of pretzel make great antlers and arms. All the materials are edible, so use your imagination! Create a holiday ornament that is a feast for the eyes as well as the palate.

4. A paper umbrella gives this s'more a very casual summertime look.

5. Clever pretzel antlers and a Red nose turn this s'more into "you know who."

6. This s'more says "I love you" with pastel candy hearts.

More S'Mores

Speaking of holidays, these little treats are perfect for holiday buffets. Talk about goodies dancing in your head! Wonderful graham crackers, chocolate and marshmallows combine to delight all your senses!

Just follow the easy directions and you'll have heavenly S'Mores in no time!

1. Melt Brown, and Green chocolate leaving some of the cracker exposed. Pour Brown onto cracker. Dribble Green chocolate on top.

2. Add jumbo marshmallows while chocolate is still warm.

Some More S'Mores -
Traditionally S'Mores are made with flat pieces of chocolate bars. But, they can also be made by pouring melted chocolate onto the graham crackers.

Make fancy S'Mores on individual plates. Arrange 2 or 3 graham crackers in center of plate, overlapping slightly. Melt brown, White and a third color of chocolate separately. Pour Brown chocolate onto crackers, leaving some cracker and plate exposed. Dribble White chocolate next, then add miniature marshmallows on and off the crackers. Using third color, dribble thinly over marshmallows, crackers and exposed plate. Try varying chocolate flavors for an added surprise!

Holiday Peppermint Bar...

1. Wrap container.

2. Tie a bow to secure wrap and treat.